E220056613

Match your theme to the 2012 EYFS

Planning for Learning through
People who help us

by Rachel Sparks Linfield and Christine Warwick. Illustrated by Cathy Hughes

Contents

Published by Practical Pre-School Books, A Division of MA Education Ltd,
St Jude's Church, Dulwich Road, Herne Hill, London, SE24 0PB Tel: 020 7738 5454

www.practicalpreschoolbooks.com

Revised (3rd edition) © MA Education Ltd 2013. Revised edition © MA Education Ltd 2008.
First edition © Step Forward Publishing Limited 2000.

Front and back cover images taken by Lucie Carlier © MA Education Ltd.

Planning for Learning through People who help us ISBN: 978-1-909280-34-2

Making plans

Child-friendly planning

The purpose of planning is to make sure that all children enjoy a broad and balanced experience of learning. Planning should be flexible, useful and child-friendly. It should reflect opportunities available both indoors and outside. Plans form part of a planning cycle in which practitioners make observations, assess and plan.

Children benefit from reflective planning that takes into account the children's current interests and abilities and also allows them to take the next steps in their learning. Plans should make provision for activity that promotes learning and a desire to imagine, observe, communicate, experiment, investigate and create.

Plans should include a variety of types of activity. Some will be adult-initiated or adult-led, that focus on key skills or concepts. These should be balanced with opportunities for child-initiated activity where the children take a key role in the planning. In addition there is a need to plan for the on-going continuous provision areas such as construction, sand and water, malleable materials, small world, listening area, role-play and mark-making. Thought also needs to be given to the enhanced provision whereby an extra resource or change may enable further exploration, development and learning.

The outdoor environment provides valuable opportunities for children's learning. It is vital that plans value the use of outdoor space.

The UK Frameworks

Within the UK a number of frameworks exist to outline the provision that children should be entitled to receive. Whilst a variety of terms and labels are used to describe the Areas of Learning there are key principles which are common to each document. For example they advocate that practitioners' planning should be personal based on observations and knowledge of the specific children within a setting. They acknowledge that young children learn best when there is scope for child-initiated activity. In addition it is accepted that young children's learning is holistic. Although within the documents Areas of Learning are presented separately to ensure that key areas are not over-looked, within settings, children's learning will combine areas. Thus the Areas of

Learning are perhaps of most use for planning, assessment and recording.

Focused area plans

The plans you make for each day will outline areas of continuous provision and focused, adult-led activities. Plans for focused-area activities need to include aspects such as:

● resources needed;
● the way in which you might introduce activities;
● individual needs;
● the organisation of adult help;
● size of the group;
● timing;
● safety;
● key vocabulary.

Identify the learning and the Early Learning Goals that each activity is intended to promote. Make a note of any assessments or observations that you are likely to carry out. After carrying out the activities, make notes on your plans to say what was particularly successful, or any changes you would make another time.

A final note

Planning should be seen as flexible. Not all groups meet every day, and not all children attend every day. Any part of the plan can be used independently, stretched over a longer period or condensed to meet the needs of any group. You will almost certainly adapt the activities as children respond to them in different ways and bring their own ideas, interests

Making plans

and enthusiasms. The important thing is to ensure that the children are provided with a varied and enjoyable curriculum that meets their individual developing needs.

Using the book

Read the section which outlines links to the Early Learning Goals (pages 4-7) and explains the rationale for focusing on 'People who help us'.

Use pages 8 to 19 to select from a wide range of themed, focused activities that recognise the importance of involving children in practical activities and giving them opportunities to follow their own interests. For each 'People who help us' theme, two activities are described in detail as examples to help you in your planning and preparation. Key vocabulary, questions and learning opportunities are identified. Use the activities as a basis to:

- extend current and emerging interests and capabilities
- engage in sustained conversations
- stimulate new interests and skills.

Find out on page 20 how the 'People who help us' activities can be brought together in a Thank You Party.

Use page 21 for ideas of resources to collect or prepare. Remember that the books listed are only suggestions. It is likely that you will already have within your setting a variety of other books that will be equally useful.

The activity overview chart on page 23 can be used either at the planning stage or after each theme has been completed. It will help you to see at a glance which aspects of children's development are being addressed and alert you to the areas which may need greater input in the future.

As children take part in the activities, their learning will progress. 'Collecting evidence' on page 22 explains how you might monitor each child's achievements.

There is additional material to support the working partnership of families and children in the form of a reproducible Family Page found inside the back cover.

It is important to appreciate that the ideas presented in this book will only be a part of your planning. Many activities that will be taking place as routine

in your group may not be mentioned. For example, it is assumed that sand, dough, water, puzzles, role-play, floor toys, technology and large scale apparatus are part of the ongoing early years experience. Role-play areas, stories, rhymes, singing, and group discussion times are similarly assumed to be happening in each week although they may not be a focus for described activities.

Using the 'Early Learning Goals'

The principles that are common to each of the United Kingdom curriculum frameworks for the early years are described on page 2. It is vital that, when planning for children within a setting, practitioners are familiar with the relevant framework's content and organisation for areas of learning. Regardless however, of whether a child attends a setting in England, Northern Ireland, Scotland or Wales they have a right to provision for all areas of learning. The children should experience activities which encourage them to develop their communication and language; personal, social, emotional, physical, mathematical and creative skills. They should have opportunities within literacy and be encouraged to understand and explore their world.

Within the Statutory Framework for the Early Years Foundation Stage (2012), Communication and Language; Physical Development and Personal, Social and Emotional Development are described as Prime Areas of Learning that are 'particularly crucial for igniting children's curiosity and enthusiasm for learning, and for building their capacity to learn, form relationships and thrive' (page 4, DfE 2012). The Specific Areas of Learning are Literacy, Mathematics, Understanding the World and Expressive Arts and Design.

For each Area of Learning the Early Learning Goals (ELGs) describe what children are expected to be able to do by the time they enter Year 1. These goals, detailed on pages 4 to 7, have been used throughout this book to show how activities relating to 'People who help us' could link to these expectations. For example, for Personal, Social and Emotional Development one aim relates to the development of children's 'self-confidence and self-awareness'. Activities suggested which provide the opportunity for children to do this have the reference

PSE1. This will enable you to see which parts of the Early Learning Goals are covered for a given theme and to plan for areas to be revisited and developed.

In addition, an activity may be carried out to develop a range of different Early Learning Goals. For example, while making collages of foods on paper plates, children will develop their knowledge of shapes as they talk about the shapes they select. In addition they will be able to use their imaginations and use skills within Expressive Arts and Design. Thus, whilst adult-focused activities may have clearly defined goals at the planning stage, it must be remembered that as children take on ideas and initiate their own learning and activities, goals may change.

The Prime Areas of Learning
Communication and Language

Listening and attention: children listen attentively in a range of situations. They listen to stories, accurately anticipating key events and respond to what they hear with relevant comments, questions or actions. They give their attention to what others say and respond appropriately, while engaged in another activity. (CL1)

Understanding: children follow instructions involving several ideas or actions. They answer 'how' and 'why' questions about their experiences and in response to stories or events. (CL2)

Speaking: children express themselves effectively, showing awareness of listeners' needs. They use past, present and future forms accurately when talking about events that have happened or are to happen in the future. They develop their own narratives and explanations by connecting ideas or events. (CL3)

The theme 'People who help us' provides many opportunities for children to enjoy listening, understanding and speaking. When the children listen to stories, or speak to people such as a dentist or person from a fire station they will develop skills for CL1. Baking following a simple recipe and making plans for the 'Thank you party' will encourage both speaking and listening as well as require the children to follow instructions. Times spent speaking about people who help us at home, to have food and to be healthy and safe will allow children to develop their understanding and provide occasions for children to ask and answer questions.

Physical Development

Moving and handling: children show good control and co-ordination in large and small movements. They move confidently in a range of ways, safely negotiating space. They handle equipment and tools effectively, including pencils for writing. (PD1)

Health and self-care: children know the importance for good health of physical exercise, and a healthy diet, and talk about ways to keep healthy and safe. They manage their own basic hygiene and personal needs successfully, including dressing and going to the toilet independently. (PD2)

'People who help us' offers many opportunities for children to enjoy movement activities and to handle tools and equipment. When children take part in a simple circuit of activities, or play 'Simon says' where the actions relate to staying healthy, they can develop and demonstrate control and co-ordination. Making fruits from playdough and collecting skittles as pretend milk bottles helps children to develop their fine motor skills. Areas such as basic hygiene and going to the toilet independently, however, will be part of on-going, daily activity and, as a result, PD2 does not appear within the described activities for Physical Development for 'People who help us'.

Personal, Social and Emotional Development

Self-confidence and self-awareness: children are confident to try new activities, and say why they like some activities more than others. They are confident to speak in a familiar group, will talk about their ideas, and will choose the resources they need for their chosen activities. They say when they do or don't need help. (PSE1)

Managing feelings and behaviour: children talk about how they and others show feelings, talk about their own and others' behaviour, and its consequences, and know that some behaviour is unacceptable. They work as part of a group or class, and understand and follow the rules. They adjust their behaviour to different situations, and take changes of routine in their stride. (PSE2)

Making relationships: children play co-operatively, taking turns with others. They take account of one another's ideas about how to organise their activity. They show sensitivity to others' needs and feelings, and form positive relationships with adults and other children. (PSE3)

'People who help us' offers many opportunities, both for child-initiated and adult-led activities, that will develop children personally, socially and emotionally. When playing in a role-play grocer's shop children have the opportunity to make relationships. When discussing safety, talking to a police officer or describing ways to be helpful at home, children can develop self-confidence and self-awareness. Role-playing being a parent allows children to manage their feelings and behaviour. Many of the areas described within the ELGs for Personal, Social and Emotional Development though, will be covered on an almost incidental basis. Any activity that involves collaboration will help children to build relationships whilst self-confidence can be promoted through activities that allow children to show initiative and follow their own trains of thought.

The specific areas of Learning
Literacy

Reading: children read and understand simple sentences. They use phonic knowledge to decode regular words and read them aloud accurately. They also read some common irregular words. They demonstrate understanding when talking with others about what they have read. (L1)

Writing: children use their phonic knowledge to write words in ways which match their spoken sounds. They also write some irregular common words. They write simple sentences

which can be read by themselves and others. Some words are spelt correctly and others are phonetically plausible. (L2)

Activities for People who help us based on well-known picture books allow the children to enjoy listening to stories and to read using both their phonic knowledge and memories of common, irregular words. Discussions of the stories will help children to understand and to develop their vocabularies. Activities, such as making 'People who help me at home' books or writing invitations for the 'Thank you party' will encourage children to explore the sounds within words and to enjoy the early stages of writing.

Mathematics

Numbers: children count reliably with numbers from 1 to 20, place them in order and say which number is one more or one less than a given number. Using quantities and objects, they add and subtract two single-digit numbers and count on or back to find the answer. They solve problems, including doubling, halving and sharing. (M1)

Shape, space and measures: children use everyday language to talk about size, weight, capacity, position, distance, time and money to compare quantities and objects and to solve problems. They recognise, create and describe patterns. They explore characteristics of everyday objects and shapes and use mathematical language to describe them. (M2)

Activities for 'People Who Help Us', provide many opportunities for children to count, to measure and to explore shape and space. Using the 'Milk van' rhyme, or games about measles and rescuing people from flats, encourage children to count and to find one less. Role-play areas such as the grocer's shop highlight the use of numbers in everyday life. Decorating pizzas and making collages of

favourite foods encourage children to use shape vocabulary. Pretending to wash up develops awareness of capacity.

Understanding the World

People and communities: children talk about past and present events in their own lives and in the lives of family members. They know that other children don't always enjoy the same things, and are sensitive to this. They know about similarities and differences between themselves and others, and among families, communities and traditions. (UW1)

The world: children know about similarities and differences in relation to places, objects, materials and living things. They talk about the features of their own immediate environment and how environments might vary from one another. They make observations of animals and plants and explain why some things occur, and talk about changes. (UW2)

Technology: children recognise that a range of technology is used in places such as homes and schools. They select and use technology for particular purposes. (UW3)

To understand their world children need times to gain knowledge, to explore and to relate what they discover to both previously held ideas and future learning. Activities relating to 'People who help us' offer valuable opportunities to discover facts about food, safety and health. When exploring ways to clean windows, how long it takes dust to form or different ways to forecast weather children will be able to make comparisons. When investigating toy ambulances and using instruments to make a noise like a siren they will notice similarities and differences. Technology will be used to make 'Thank you' certificates and when considering forecasts. In addition, technology may also feature in role-play as well as being part of the on-going, daily provision.

Expressive Arts and Design

Exploring and using media and materials: children sing songs, make music and dance, and experiment with ways of changing them. They safely use and explore a variety of materials, tools and techniques, experimenting with colour, design, texture, form and function. (EAD1)

Being imaginative: children use what they have learnt about media and materials in original ways, thinking about uses and purposes. They represent their own ideas, thoughts and feelings through design and technology, art, music, dance, role-play and stories. (EAD2)

Whilst involved in activities for People Who Help Us, children will experience working with a variety of materials, tools and techniques as they paint pictures of people who buy or sell food, make tissue paper thank you button holes

and print with sponges. A number of well known songs have
been recommended which, with the addition of actions
and percussion, allow the children to be imaginative.
Collaborating to make a giant patchwork of food labels and
decorating a bedroom made in a box encourage children
to explore colour and design. Throughout all the activities
children should be encouraged to talk about what they
see and feel as they communicate their ideas in painting,
collage, music and role-play.

Note

The Early Learning Goals raise awareness of key aspects
within any child's development for each Area of Learning.
It is important to remember that these goals are reached
through a combination of adult and child-initiated activity
within Early Years settings and also a child's home life. Thus,
it is vital that goals are shared by practitioners and parents,
and children are given every opportunity to develop
throughout their Early Years Foundation Stage at home and
within a setting.

Theme 1: People who help us at home

Communication and Language

- Talk about 'People who help us at home'. Discuss what they do. Encourage children to draw pcitures of the people who help them at home. Mount the pictures and display them on a board headed with the words 'This week we would like to thank these people for helping us'. In future weeks the display can be changed as different people are mentioned and the previous display pictures made into a 'People who help us at/to...' class book. (CL1)
- Look at pictures of homes. Talk about all the jobs that have to be done to look after homes. Discuss the variety of cleaning, decorating and gardening tasks and the ways children might be able to help. Which jobs do children enjoy doing? (CL3)

Physical Development

- Play a game in which children are delivering bean-bag post. Encourage them to aim at a variety of high and low targets and to deliver their post quickly and safely. (PD1)
- Tell a story in which a parent gets up and has a busy day ahead at home doing the spring cleaning. Encourage children to listen carefully to the tale and to mime and move in time with the words. (PD1)

Personal, Social and Emotional Development

- Discuss the different things that children can do to be helpful at home. Talk about cutlery and crockery, the safe way to carry them and how to set a table. Encourage children to take it in turns to role play being a parent and setting a table for their family. (PSE2)

Literacy

- Help children to make individual 'People who help me at home' books in the shape of a house (see activity opposite). (L2)
- Look at a picture of a person who delivers mail. Talk about the way they help people to keep in touch. Enjoy sharing *The Jolly Postman or Other People's Letters* by Janet and Allan Ahlberg and looking at all the postcards and letters that the postman delivered. Provide a selection of envelopes and a variety of papers and cards for children to use for independent writing and role play. (L1, 2)
- Help children to write labels for their pictures of people who help them at home. Use the labels to begin to make the class big book. (L2)

Mathematics

- Talk about the way dishes are washed up at home. Encourage children to enjoy pretending to wash up a variety of containers in the water tray and to compare their sizes and the amounts of water that they can hold. (M2)
- Use sticky, regular shapes to make collages on paper plates of favourite foods that they eat at home. Encourage children to use shape vocabulary as they select shapes and to talk about their relative sizes. Invite children to help in displaying the plates and to talk about the people who make their meals at home and the things which children can do to help. (M2)

Understanding the World

- Look at some pictures of homes with many windows. Talk about window cleaning and the way some people have window cleaners to look after their windows. As a group investigate the best way to polish a window. Ensure that the window is safe and then compare dry and wet cloths, and soap with no soap. Some people use newspapers to polish windows. Does it work? (UW2)
- Many people use the internet or watch a weather forecast on a television before they go out. Discuss how helpful weather forecasters are and investigate different ways to forecast the weather including popular sayings. (UW3)

Expressive Arts and Design

- Paint portraits of the people who help children at home. Use pasta to decorate the edge of large sheets of card. When dry, spray the pasta with gold or silver paint and use the pasta frames to display the portraits. (EAD1)
- Encourage children to enjoy playing in the home corner and to take on a variety of roles. Talk about how it feels to be a person helping at home. (EAD2)
- Make and decorate a bedroom from a cereal packet (see activity opposite). (EAD2)

Activity: Making 'People who help me at home' books

Learning opportunity: Making books and writing names.

Early Learning Goal: Literacy. Writing.

Resources: Crayons; pencils; a picture book; for each child a book made from a piece of A4 card folded in half and cut in the shape of a house with a piece of A4 paper stapled inside.

Key vocabulary: Help, helpful, names of people, author, illustrator.

Organisation: Small group.

What to do: Remind children of the discussions about people who help them at home. Show them the house-shaped books and explain that they are each going to make a book about the people who help them at home. Show the children the pages and together count them.

Ask children to say who they would like to draw in their books. Give each child a book and ask them to begin to draw one of the people they have suggested on the first page. Encourage them to put in details so that the person can be identified and to write the person's name on the page. Help them to write a sentence about each person.

When all four pages have been completed, decorate the covers with windows, a door and roof tiles. Show children a picture book, point out the author's and illustrator's names and explain that they are authors and illustrators. Encourage them to write their own names on their books.

Activity: Making cereal packet bedrooms

Learning opportunity: Making model bedrooms using a range of materials.

Early Learning Goal: Expressive Arts and Design. Being imaginative.

Resources: Small boxes, cotton reels, shells, cardboard tubes, carpet scraps, wallpaper, paper, fabric, paint; scissors; glue; cereal packets turned inside out with one large face removed.

Key vocabulary: Names for rooms in a house and bedroom furniture, wallpaper, carpet.

Organisation: Whole group introduction, small group activity.

What to do: Remind children of the discussion they had about all the jobs that need to be done in a home. Talk about decorating rooms and the different ways this can be done. Who has wallpaper in their bedroom? Who has paint?

Show children a cereal packet that has had one large face removed. Ask children to shut their eyes and to imagine that the box is their bedroom. What would they like to put in their room? How would they like to decorate it? Invite children to share their ideas and to look at samples of wallpapers.

Break up into smaller groups according to whether children wish to paint their room, to make wallpaper or use felt pens and crayons.

In follow-up sessions children could talk about floor covering and use scraps of carpet, fabric or paper to complete the decorating. Finally, furniture made from small boxes, cotton reels, shells or cardboard tubes and so on could be added.

Display

On a large noticeboard display the pictures of people who help children at home with the heading 'This week we would like to thank these people for helping us!' On a nearby table put out a book box of non-fiction books about people who help children. As the display is changed each week and big books are made with the pictures taken down, add the class books to the display.

On another board put up the cereal packet rooms in groups to form houses. Use corrugated card and textured papers to make roofs for the houses and ask children to suggest a name for the street.

Display the paper plates of food on a table covered with a tablecloth along with plastic play cutlery and beakers for children to practise setting tables.

Theme 2: People who help us at school/nursery/pre-school

Communication and Language

- Ask children to suggest the names of all the people who help them at school/nursery/pre-school. Encourage them to think about the people who clean, who make meals, who look after the books, who set out activities and who answer the telephone. Talk about what would happen if one of the people was ill and could not do their work. Help the children to appreciate that each person has an important role. (CL3)
- Make finger puppets from card circles of the people who help at school. Enjoy using the puppets to talk about what the people have done to be helpful and what they hope to do. Collaborate in playing with the puppets. (CL3)

Physical Development

- Talk about the routines that are helpful when playing outside with large toys, such as stopping for a whistle or bell. Enjoy playing outside with large toys and encourage children to be helpful and also to appreciate how the adults that watch help them. (PD1)
- Talk about the rules that are necessary for using large apparatus safely. How do these rules help the teacher? How do the rules help children? Enjoy using large apparatus. Encourage children to understand both how they are helped and how they can help. (PD1)

Personal, Social and Emotional Development

- Ask children to make a portrait of someone who helps them at school/nursery/pre-school. Encourage children to choose their own materials and techniques.(PSE1)
- Ask children to suggest ways that they could help those who help them. Talk about the importance of being tidy and putting toys away in their correct places. Demonstrate how to clean a table with a damp cloth and how to use a dustpan and brush. Encourage children to be helpful and to think about how their actions affect others. (PSE2)

Literacy

- Turn the book corner into a library. Invite children to help to make tickets for books, labels for shelves/boxes and posters to show where different books are kept. Talk about the difference between non-fiction and fiction books. During the week encourage children to take it in turns to be a librarian and to run the group's library. (L2)
- Read *Mr Tick the Teacher* by Allan Ahlberg and Faith Jaques. Is Mr Tick similar to teachers that the group know? Would children like to be taught by Mr Tick? All of Mr Tick's children's names begin with 't'. As a group make a word bank of names that begin with 't'. (L2)
- Read a story about a child going to school for the first time such as *Billy and the Big New School* by Catherine and Laurence Anholt or 'In which Sophie Goes to School' in *Sophie's Tom* by Dick King-Smith. Talk about the reasons why the children were worried about going to school and the things that they looked forward to. What helped the children to be happy to go to school? Make a welcome letter for a new child. (L2)

Mathematics

- Remind children of the discussion about putting toys away in their correct places. Provide children with baskets of shapes and ask them to help you to sort them. As children sort, encourage them to talk about the shapes, the number of edges/faces and their names. Ask children to make labels for the baskets and to count how many shapes are in each container. (M1, 2)
- Play the library game (see activity opposite).(M1)

Understanding the World

- Talk about the jobs that have to be done each day to keep the room clean. Investigate how long it takes for dust to form (see activity opposite). (UW2)
- Invite an adult known to the children to come and talk about their memories of school. Who were the people who helped them? What did they do to help their teachers and other adults? (UW1)
- Help children to look closely at their surroundings and to notice how furniture is arranged and where things are kept. Encourage them to compare these observations with a picture of a classroom in the past with children seated in rows, writing on slates. Help them to notice people's expressions and to think about how it might have felt to be at school then. Who would have helped those schoolchildren? (UW2)

Expressive Arts and Design

- Help children to draw around one of their hands and to cut it out. Decorate the hands with drawings of children or adults being helpful. Use the hands as leaves on a 'helping hand tree'. (EAD1)
- Enjoy using tuned and untuned percussion to make a 'tidy up' song or tune. Record the music and play it during tidying up times. (EAD1)
- Set out the role-play area with a small blackboard and chalk; a variety of pens, crayons, pencils and papers; books and so on. Invite children to take it in turns to be the teacher and to enjoy helping their pupils. (EAD2)

Activity: The library game

Learning opportunity: Counting to ten and recognising numerals to nine.

Early Learning Goal: Mathematics. Numbers.

Resources: Two sets of tickets with the numerals one to nine and four blank cards; 18 books with tickets (self-stick notes) with numerals one to nine.

Key vocabulary: Numbers one to nine, library, book, ticket.

Organisation: Small group.

What to do: Talk about the way librarians look after the books in a library and help people to borrow them.

Show children the books and the numbers attached to each one. Explain that they are going to take it in turn to select a ticket and borrow the book which matches the ticket. Shuffle the number cards and put them number side down in the centre of the group. Invite children in turn to take a number card and match it to a book. (The blank card means miss a turn.)

The game is finished when all the books have been borrowed. The winner is the person who has collected the most books.

Activity: Investigating dust

Learning opportunity: Observing and comparing.

Early Learning Goal: Understanding the World. The world.

Resources: Duster; square of white card 10 x 10 cm; shelf or table which can remain untouched for up to a week.

Key vocabulary: Dust, clean.

Organisation: Whole group.

What to do: Talk about dust and the way it gathers in places. Clear a shelf or table and invite children to help to clean it with a damp duster. Tell them that although the furniture has been cleaned dust will come back. Invite the children to help you to find out how long it takes for dust to form. Explain that in order to do the experiment the furniture must not be touched or disturbed.

Lay the card square in the centre of the cleaned surface. Each morning, inspect the furniture with the children. When dust has appeared, remove the card square and help children to compare the clean, protected area with the dust-covered surface. Allow each child to run a finger over the dust to both see and feel it. Also, compare the dusty card with a clean piece. Finally, talk about the cleaning jobs which are carried out at school/nursery/pre-school and help children to appreciate why they take place at regular intervals.

Display

Cut out a large tree trunk and branches from brown sugar paper. Display it at floor height so that children feel it is a real tree. Stick the helping hands on the branches. Nearby put out a basket of extra paper hands and during the week encourage children to add more helping hands of things that they have noticed others doing to help them. Cut out a large 't' from paper. On this write all the 't' names that children suggested. Invite children to suggest and write more 't' words to fill the letter.

Theme 3: People who help keep us safe

Communication and Language
- Invite a school crossing patrol person to talk to the group about their job and how to cross roads safely. (CL1)
- Invite a person from the local fire station to come and talk to children about their job and how they help people. (Some stations may be willing to bring a fire engine to the group whilst others may run open days during the year.) (CL1)

Physical Development
- Play the traffic light game in which colours indicate what children need to do. (Green means walk, amber means hop and red means stand absolutely still.) As you play the game, say the colours with different expression to encourage children to listen to what is said and not simply the way it is said. (PD1)
- Talk about how important it is to listen when you cross the road. Practise listening skills by playing 'The keeper of the keys'. A blindfolded child sits on a chair in the middle of a circle of children seated on the floor. Under the chair is a bunch of keys. In turn children try to tiptoe and take the keys. The keeper stops the keys being taken by pointing to where they hear a sound. Each keeper is allowed to point three times before another keeper is chosen. (PD1)

Personal, Social and Emotional Development
- Talk about safety and what children can do to help themselves. Encourage them to realise that although there are many people who help them to be safe they also have their parts to play. (PSE2)
- Invite a police officer to talk to the group about the things that they do to help people to be safe and the things children should do to help themselves. Record the visit with photographs. (PSE2, 3)

Literacy
- Talk about people who help children to cross the road safely and 'stop/go' signs. Provide card circles, straws and pens for children to make their own signs. Encourage them to write and read the words and use the signs in role-play. (L1, 2)

- Talk about sun safety and what parents and carers can do to help protect their children. Make sun saftety posters or leaflets. (L2)

Mathematics
- Ask children to make houses with windows from construction toys, to compare their heights and to make ladders to rescue play people (see activity opposite). (M2)
- On a large sheet of paper draw a block of flats with six floors. On each floor draw two windows and put a play person in each window. Play a game in which children pretend to be a firefighter rescuing people. In order to rescue a person a dice is thrown and a person is collected from the corresponding floor. As the game is played, encourage children to count the floors, the empty windows, the number of people rescued and how many more people need to be rescued to empty the building. (M1)

Understanding the World
- Examine a pushchair to look at safety straps. Talk about how they work. Provide boxes, ribbon, wool etc. for children to make safe pushchairs or chairs for a teddy. (UW2)

- Show children the safety warning on a toy which states that it is only suitable for children over the age of three years due to the presence of small parts which could be swallowed. Examine a selection of toys and sort them according to whether they would be safe for very young children. Some children may like to use cardboard tubes as a way to decide whether a toy or part is too small. Toys which can pass through the tube would be too tiny. Talk about the safety checks which toy factories would carry out to help to keep children safe. (UW2)

Expressive Arts and Design

- Show children a picture of a police officer directing traffic and one of people using lights to cross a road. Ask children to make lights to help people to cross a road (see activity opposite). (EAD2)
- Set out an area as a town with roads, zebra and pelican crossings, fire, police and ambulance stations and a variety of play people and vehicles. Encourage children to enjoy playing in the town and to be people who help others to be safe. Provide signpost shapes cut from card, crayons and pencils and encourage children to make signs which could help people to be safe. (EAD2)
- Enjoy putting actions and percussion to songs and poems which feature people who help to keep us safe such as 'The fireman' in Apusskido: Songs for Children and 'London's Burning' (traditional). (EAD1)

Activity: Making fire-engine ladders

Learning opportunity: Comparing heights and talking about lengths and positions.

Early Learning Goal: Mathematics. Shape, space and measures.

Resources: Houses made from construction toys; strips of card; scissors; glue; toy fire engine with a ladder.

Key vocabulary: Taller, smaller, shorter, shortest, tallest, higher, lower, ladder, rescue.

Organisation: Small group.

What to do: Arrange the houses previously made from construction toys in a row and place a play person on each roof. Show children a toy fire engine with a ladder and talk about the way it can be used to rescue people from fires. Show children the street of houses and ask which one would need the longest ladder to rescue the person on the roof. As a group, arrange the houses in order of height. Finally, help children to make a ladder for each house from two strips of card with card rungs glued on. Throughout the work encourage children to compare lengths and heights and to describe where the people are positioned.

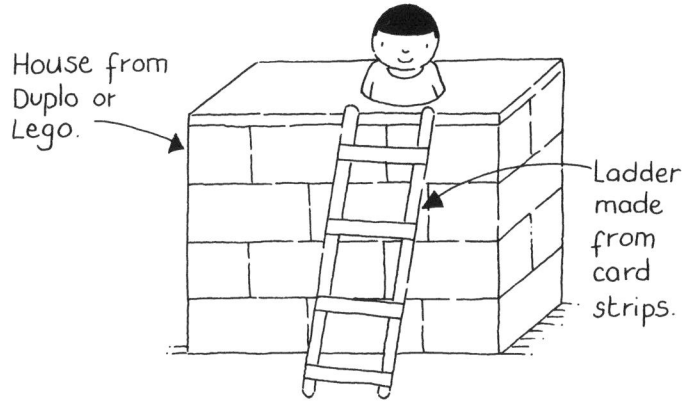

House from Duplo or Lego.

Ladder made from card strips.

Activity: Making pelican crossing lights

Learning opportunity: Using a range of materials to construct pelican crossing lights.

Early Learning Goal: Expressive Arts and Design. Being imaginative.

Resources: Lolly sticks; cardboard tubes, straws; balsa wood; red and green cotton reels; red and green paper and cellophane; plastic pots; Plasticine; glue; picture of people using a pelican crossing.

Key vocabulary: Red, green, pelican crossing, safe.

Organisation: Small group.

What to do: Talk to children about crossing the road. Where are the safest places to cross? Look at the picture of the pelican crossing and ask what the different lights mean. When can people cross the road? When must they not cross?

Invite children to make a pelican crossing. Show the group the resources. Ask the children to shut their eyes, to imagine what they are going to make and to raise a hand when they have an idea. Once all hands have been raised, ask them to explain what they are going to do. Encourage children to share ideas and to help friends to solve problems as they begin to carry out their constructing. When the lights have been finished, use them for play activities with toy cars and dolls.

Display

Display the photographs from the police officer visit on a board with captions written by the children. On a table put out the sun safety leaflets with clean empty bottles from sunscreen. Behind, arrange the sun safety posters.

Theme 4:
People who help keep us healthy

Communication and Language

- Talk about how it feels to be unwell and the people who help to make us feel better. (Check beforehand that no child will be upset. Some family health problems could make this too sensitive an area for some children.) (CL3)
- Tell the traditional tale of 'Jack and the Beanstalk'. Later in the week read to them the story of *Jim and the Beanstalk* by Raymond Briggs in which Jim helps the giant to have new teeth, glasses and a wig. Talk about the people who helped the giant to be healthier. (CL1)
- Invite a dentist to talk to the group about the way dentists help people to take care of their teeth and the importance of cleaning teeth. Talk about the way that sugary foods can harm them. Use a sand timer to demonstrate how long teeth should be brushed for each morning and evening. Ask children to make 'Clean your teeth!' posters. (CL1)

Physical Development

- Encourage children to move quickly and to enjoy running and jumping in a large space. Following the session, help children to notice the way their bodies change when they are active. Talk about the importance of taking exercise to be healthy. (PD1, 2)
- Talk to children about the way athletes and footballers often do circuit training to help to keep their bodies

healthy. Make a simple circuit of activities such as walking along a bench, rolling a ball, jumping in and out of hoops and so on. Encourage children to use the circuit and to remember the instructions for each piece or set of equipment. (PD1)
- Play 'Simon says' in which all the actions are related to staying healthy such as peeling an apple, combing hair, washing hands, brushing teeth and going for a run. (PD2)

Personal, Social and Emotional Development

- Contact a local hospital or doctor's surgery and enquire whether they would like a frieze to decorate an area. As a group, talk about the importance of thanking those people who help to keep us healthy. Discuss what could go on the frieze and involve all children in making it. Once displayed, take a photo so that children can see where their work has gone. (PSE3)

Literacy

- Sing 'Miss Polly had a dolly who was sick, sick, sick' from *Okki-tokki-unga: Action Songs for Chidren* chosen by Beatrice Harrop, Linda Friend and David Gadsby. Talk about how the dolly felt and who looked after her. Provide paper, crayons and pencils for the children to write bills for the doctor and to make 'Get Well' cards for the doll. (L2)
- Involve children in making letter charts for a role-play optician's. Display the charts in a corner and invite children to take it in turns to be a customer or an optician. Encourage them to use the charts, talk on the telephone, make appointments in a diary and write customer reminders and bills for glasses. Provide a selection of plastic sun and play spectacles. (L2)

Mathematics

- Play the measles game (see activity opposite). (M1)
- Use nine ambulances made from card and numbered from one to nine for number recognition and ordering activities. (M1)

Understanding the World

- Ambulances which rush to emergencies have sirens and lights. Show children a picture of an ambulance

and talk about the way the siren and light help people to know where ambulances are. Provide a range of percussion instruments and investigate which ones sound most like a siren. Which instruments would be most useful for warning people? (UW2)

- Compare a selection of toy ambulances. Help the children to make ambulances with moving wheels from boxes turned inside out, cotton reels, dowelling, plastic tubing and clothes pegs (see diagram below). (UW2)

Expressive Arts and Design

- Make a variety of hairstyles by trimming hair made from sugar paper attached to paper-plate faces (see activity to the right). (EAD1)
- Talk about people who take X-rays. Discuss how X-rays are used to show broken bones and how the bones can be set in plaster to help them mend. Read Funnybones by Janet and Allan Ahlberg. Make X-rays with white paint on black paper or by sticking white straw pieces on black card. (EAD1)
- Make dolls from wooden spoons with two faces, one that is sad and unwell and one that is happy and healthy. Encourage children to use their dolls whilst singing 'Miss Polly had a dolly who was sick, sick, sick'. (EAD2)

Activity: The measles game

Learning opportunity: Counting to ten and comparing numbers.

Early Learning Goal: Mathematics. Numbers.

Resources: Red counters; faces drawn on large paper plates; a dice numbered one to six; a box lined with felt in which to throw the dice.

Key vocabulary: Spot, measles, numbers one to ten, more, fewer, fewest, most.

Organisation: Small group.

What to do: Give each child a paper face and ten counters. Ask them to check how many counters they have and to lay

them out on their plate face. Explain that the people have measles and they are going to be the nurses who help to make them better. Invite children to take it in turn to roll the dice and to remove the number of spots indicated. After each go encourage children to say how many spots they had, how many they have taken away and the number that are left. The game finishes when no spots remain.

Activity: Cutting paper hair

Learning opportunity: Using scissors.

Early Learning Goal: Expressive Arts and Design Exploring and using media and materials.

Resources: For each child a paper plate with long strips of sugar paper firmly stapled on as hair to be trimmed; scissors; felt pens.

Key vocabulary: Hair, long, short, curly, straight, hairdresser, cut, trim.

Organisation: Small group.

What to do: Remind children of the importance of looking after their hair and the way that people who trim and wash our hair help us to do this. Provide each child with a paper-plate head with hair made from long strips of sugar paper. Ask children to pretend that they are hairdressers and to trim the hair on the paper-plate heads. Remind children that once cut the hair cannot be glued back on! Show children how by wrapping the paper around their fingers firmly the hair can be helped to wave. To finish, give each head a face. Remind children where to position eyes.

Note: Because paper plates tend to have a waxy surface, this activity works best if the back of the plate is used as the face.

Display

Make a sign that says 'For healthy hair come to ....'s hair salon'. Use border paper to create a shop window effect. Arrange the group's paper hairstyles in the 'window'. Use the town layout made during Theme 3 to display the box ambulances. On a nearby table put out the measles game for children to play with during free play. Stick the X-rays on windows, if possible, along with a real X-ray. Nearby put out a plastic model or poster of a skeleton.

Theme 5: People who help us to have food

Communication and Language
- Show children the ingredients for a cake or biscuits. Talk about where they came from and help children to realise that many stages come before a product is sold in a shop. (CL1)
- Help children to follow a simple recipe to make biscuits. (Check first for children's food allergies and area health and safety guidelines for cooking activities.) (CL2)

Physical Development
- Observe a range of fruits and make fruits from playdough. (PD1)
- Use skittles as milk bottles for races. Set out skittles in rows and ask children to collect the 'empty bottles'. Carry out simple relays in which a skittle is 'delivered'. (PD1)
- Outside use wheeled vehicles to be people delivering food. (PD1)

Personal, Social and Emotional Development
- Invite a shopkeeper, milk delivery person, gardener, farmer, baker and/or cook to talk about how they help people to have food and what they do. Before the visits discuss with children the types of questions that they might ask. (PSE1, 3)
- Together set up the role-play area as a grocery store with posters, price lists, a toy cash register, play foods, paper bags, plastic baskets and money. Encourage children to enjoy buying and selling food. (PSE3)

Literacy
- Make posters to advertise foods on sale in a role-play shop. (L2)
- Read *Oliver's Fruit Salad* or/and *Oliver's Vegetables* by Vivian French. Make concertina flap books of favourite fruits or vegetables (see activity opposite). (L1, 2)
- Use pictures of foods for matching to their initial sounds and for playing 'Find the food which is delivered by/sold by/comes from...'. (L2)

Mathematics
- Use the 'Milk van' counting rhyme (see activity opposite). (M1)
- Use the favourite food concertina flap books for counting activities. (M1)
- Make pizzas to investigate shape. For example decorate them with triangles of ham, and circles of tomato. When decorated count the number of even shape on the pizza. (M1, 2)

Understanding the World
- Investigate which fruits can be grown from pips. Encourage children to collect pips from fruit they eat at home and plant them. (UW2)
- Enjoy looking at the pictures in a book about farming such as *1001 Things to Spot on the Farm* by Gillian Doherty. Help children to notice all the things which farmers have to do to grow crops and look after animals. Encourage children to ask questions and to enjoy discovering facts about the way farmers help to provide food. (UW2)

Expressive Arts and Design
- Make a large patchwork of clean food labels. During the week ask children to collect labels from all the foods that they eat and to stick them on to a large noticeboard so that all spaces are filled. Encourage children to think about the shape and colour of each label and where it would look best in the patchwork. (EAD1)
- Use sponges cut in the shape of fruits and vegetables or firm fruits and vegetables and ready-mixed paint for printing. The prints are especially effective if done on black sugar paper. (EAD1)

● Look at pictures of food markets. Look at the types of foods that are sold and how they are arranged on the stalls. Invite children to paint large portraits of people buying or selling food to go on a group frieze of a market. Also involve children in the painting of fruits and vegetables to cut out for the stalls. (EAD1)

Activity: Making concertina flap books

Learning opportunity: Making books and writing initial sounds, and words.

Early Learning Goal: Literacy. Reading, writing.

Resources: Copies of *Oliver's Fruit Salad* or/and *Oliver's Vegetables* by Vivian French; for each child a concertina flap book made from a folded sheet of A4 sized card (see diagram); pencils; crayons.

Key vocabulary: Book, page, author, names of fruits and vegetables, author, illustrator.

Organisation: Small group.

What to do: On a previous day together read either or both the Oliver books. Before introducing the concertina books talk about fruits and vegetables that children like and why they taste special. Look at the pictures in the Oliver books and encourage the children to consider why Oliver did not initially like certain foods and how his grandparents helped him to like them.

Show children the concertina books and explain that they are each going to make a book about their favourite vegetables and fruits. Show how to lift the flaps and explain that the food will be drawn under the flap. Ask children to tell you what they would like to draw and check that they are aware of the shapes and colours of the fruits and vegetables.

When all drawings and colouring has been completed help the children to write the initial letter for each fruit and vegetable on the flaps, and the word underneath. Remind the children that they are the authors and illustrators and their names should be on their books. Later in the week use the books to play 'I spy a fruit/vegetable under the flap that begins with ......'

Activity: The milk van counting rhyme

Learning opportunity: Counting to ten.

Early Learning Goal: Mathematics. Numbers.

Resources: None.

Key vocabulary: Numbers ten to zero, crate, milk, bottle, van.

Organisation: Whole group.

What to do: Recite the following rhyme to the group, showing the actions and encouraging children to join in with the counting. As the rhyme progresses children are likely to join in with the words and the actions.

I met a milk van	*(with arms mime wheels)*
With <u>ten</u> cartons in a crate.	*(show ten fingers)*
I bought <u>one</u> carton	*(put down one finger)*
The milk tasted great!	*(mime drinking milk)*
That left <u>nine</u> cartons on the van.	*(show and count nine fingers)*

Later in the day repeat the rhyme but with children taking a greater part in the reciting and counting. On further occasions the rhyme could include a child with ten washed-out milk cartons or skittles to deliver; throw a dice numbered from nought to two to govern how many cartons can be bought each time.

Display

Involve children in displaying their food labels to make the large patchwork and in providing the background for the market frieze. Use large brushes or sponges to paint the sky and ground for the market. Make stalls from cardboard boxes and place these in front of the board. Invite children to position their market traders and shoppers and to help in arranging the painted fruits and vegetables on the stalls. Mount the fruit and vegetable prints on brightly coloured paper and combine them to make a second large patchwork. Use the patchworks for counting activities. In a nearby basket place the concertina flap books.

Planning
for
Learning
through
**People who
help us**

17

Theme 6: The thank you party

Communication and Language
- Explain to the children that there is going to be a party to say thank you to all the people that they have been thinking about over the past few weeks. Talk about the preparations needed. (CL1)
- Read a story about a party such as *Alfie and the Birthday Surprise* by Shirley Hughes. Ask children why the surprise party was planned and how it helped to cheer up Bob MacNally. Talk about the preparations that took place for the party and the ones the children will need to make for their thank-you party. (CL1)

Physical Development
- Play the thank you ball-rolling game (see activity opposite). (PD1)
- Encourage children to travel around, under, over and through balancing and climbing equipment in the role of a helping person who has been mentioned during the topic. Examples could include a milk delivery person who stops at each piece of equipment to leave milk, a market stall holder who carries imaginary boxes, a police officer who moves quickly and safely between equipment and a window cleaner who climbs to polish windows. (PD1)

Personal, Social and Emotional Development
- Use the big books that children have made as the stimulus for making a list of people that children would like to invite to the thank you party. (PSE1)
- During a circle time encourage children to complete the sentence 'I want to thank .... because..'. (PSE3)

Literacy
- Encourage children to make up stories about some of the people who visited and to write their ideas. Use the stories in a group 'big book'. Show children some picture books which have dedications. Explain what a dedication is and dedicate the group's book to the people who help them. (L2)
- Involve children in the making of invitations for the party. Help them to fill in the name of the person being invited and the group's name. (L2)

Mathematics
- Use the party as the stimulus for counting activities. Count the number of people who are invited, the number of people who say they can come, the number of thank you certificates that need to be made, and so on. (M1)
- Enjoy replaying games used within the People Who Help Us topic. Invite children to choose their favourite games and also to think about how the rules could be altered to make a new game. (M – depends on the games chosen)
- Involve children in making a number frieze of pictures associated with the people that are to be thanked. For instance, the frieze could be of one nurse, two farmers, three nurses and so on, or it might be of objects such as one fire engine, two milk cartons, three envelopes, four rubbish sacks and so on. Encourage children to suggest ideas for the number frieze. (M1)

Understanding the World
- On a computer make thank you certificates. Involve children in selecting the font, colour and decoration. Talk about the way that the computer is useful for producing a large number of certificates quickly and the ease with which text and pictures can be altered. (UW3)
- Make shakers from rice and plastic tubs to accompany the thank you song (see Expressive Arts and Design). (UW2)

- Show children pictures of a variety of parties such as street parties, birthday parties and so on. Talk about the occasions for which parties are held including ones from a range of cultures. (UW1)

Expressive Arts and Design

- Play 'The farmer's in his den' (traditional) but change the words to include the people who children have been thinking about (for example 'The teacher's in her school; The doctor's in her surgery; The driver's in his bus'). Encourage children to move in time with the words and to invent actions for each of the characters. (EAD1)
- Practise the 'Thanking day song' (see activity right). (EAD1)
- Write each of the letters in 'thank you' on large sheets of card or stiff paper. Divide the children into small groups and give a letter to each one. Encourage the children to decorate their letters. Use them to make a thank you banner. (EAD1)
- Use tissue-paper circles, green plastic straws, clear tape, green paper leaves and silver foil to make thank you button holes (see diagram above). (EAD1)

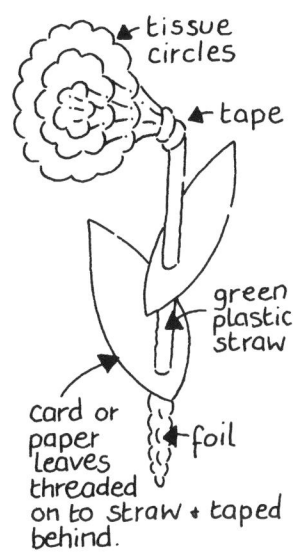

tissue circles

tape

green plastic straw

card or paper leaves threaded on to straw + taped behind.

foil

Activity: The thank you ball-rolling game

Learning opportunity: Rolling balls and playing a collaborative game.

Early Learning Goal: Physical Development. Moving and handling.

Resources: A variety of large and small plastic and sponge balls.

Key vocabulary: Names of people in the group, roll, ball, thank you.

Organisation: Whole group sitting on the floor in a circle.

What to do: Demonstrate to the group how a ball can be rolled across the circle. Show children how to aim the ball and how to push it hard enough to reach someone but not so hard that it goes out of the circle. Once all children have had the chance to practise rolling a ball, ask them to stand up, still in the circle. Explain that they are each going to have a turn at rolling the ball. Before sending the ball they must say 'I'm going to send the ball to ....'. After they have rolled the ball they should sit down. Try the

activity several times, encouraging children to keep an eye on the ball, to send it quickly and to sit quietly.

Challenge the children to complete the circle rolling before you have counted to a certain number or before the sand has gone through a sand timer. On other occasions repeat the activity and as well as naming the person who is to receive the ball ask children to say 'Thank you .... for ....'.

Before starting, talk about the sorts of things children might wish to say thank you for. Changing the size of the ball can add further variety.

Activity: The thanking day song

Learning opportunity: Singing and playing percussion instruments.

Early Learning Goal: Expressive Arts and Design. Exploring and using media and materials.

Resources: Shakers.

Key vocabulary: Words for the song, loud, louder, soft, quietly.

Organisation: Whole group sitting on the floor.

What to do: To the tune of 'Happy birthday to you' sing the 'Thanking day' song.

Happy thanking day to you,
Happy thanking day to you,
We want to say thank you
For all that you do!

Explain to the children that this song will be sung at the thank you party for all the people the children want to thank. Teach the words of the song to the group. Show children how the speed can be changed and the volume. Say that the song should sound happy and ask children to suggest how it should be sung. Hand out the shakers and let children experiment with the ways that they can be played. Finally, sing the song once without shakers and once with them to produce a grand finale.

Display

Hang the thank you banner in a prominent position to welcome people to the party. Check displays for loose corners and pieces which may have come adrift. Set out all the books that have been made during the topic. Line baskets with green crêpe paper and arrange the button holes ready to present to people at the thank you party.

Bringing it all together

The thank you party

Before starting the People who help us activities, alert those who will be invited to the party of the date and ask whether they are likely to be able to attend. In this way, planning can take place for approximate numbers and children will be saved from too many rejections!

Preparation

Explain to the children that the purpose of the party is to say thank you to their families, friends and people who have visited. Talk about how it feels to be thanked and ask for suggestions for the kinds of things that might happen at the party.

With the children plan and practise a small presentation in which they can show things they have made, recite rhymes and sing songs.

Allocate jobs so that all children have something special to do. This might be presenting the button holes and certificates, handing around food or welcoming people with an adult.

Food

No party is complete without food but the type and amount is likely to depend on the number of people expected to attend. Possible foods include:

- slices of apple dunked in melted chocolate
- egg baskets made from cornflakes, melted chocolate and mini chocolate eggs
- savoury biscuits
- gingerbread people iced as police, nurses and so on
- drink made from a mixture of fruit juices and lemonade.

For an extra special party feeling straws could be decorated by children using small pieces of card with two slits for the straw to slip through (see diagram).

The party

Start the party with the presentation by the children. Ensure that items by individual children are balanced with ones by the whole group. Doing this reduces the urge to fidget! Involve all children in reciting rhymes, singing the 'Happy thanking day' song and playing their shakers. Finally, invite children to give to each person present their thank you certificate and paper flower button-hole.

Following the giving of certificates and button-holes, ask people to remain seated whilst children, with adults to supervise, hand round the food and drinks. To finish invite the guests to look around the displays and to participate in a quiz. Prepare, on one side of A4 paper, 20 simple questions for an adult to complete with a child. Include questions to do with the presentation, the food and the displays. Provide each pair with the quiz and a pencil and give small prizes for completed quizzes.

Resources

Resources to collect

- Clothes to role-play being 'people who help us' such as nurses, police and bakers.
- Toys for role-play areas such as shops, cafes and opticians.
- Poster or plastic model of a human skeleton.
- An X-ray or picture of an X-ray of a human bone.
- Wooden spoons.
- Toy ambulances

Everyday resources

- Cereal packets and shoe boxes
- Variety of papers and cards such as sugar, tissue, silver and shiny papers, wallpaper and corrugated card
- Paint, different sized paint brushes and a variety of paint mixing containers
- A variety of pencils, crayons, pastels and felt pens
- Glue and scissors
- Decorative and finishing materials such as sequins, foils, glitter, tinsel, shiny wool and threads, beads, pieces of textiles and parcel ribbon
- Table covers
- Malleable materials such as play-dough
- Green plastic straws
- Plastic cotton reels
- Pasta

Stories

- *Topsy and Tim Go to the Doctor* by Jean and Gareth Adamson
- *Topsy and Tim Have Itchy Heads* by Jean and Gareth Adamson
- *Topsy and Tim Meet the Firefighters* by Jean and Gareth Adamson
- *Topsy and Tim Safety First* by Jean and Gareth Adamson
- *Topsy and Tim Start School* by Jean and Gareth Adamson
- *Funnybones* by Janet and Allan Ahlberg
- *Mr Tick the Teacher* by Janet and Allan Ahlberg
- *The Jolly Postman* by Janet and Allan Ahlberg
- *Billy and the Big New School* by Catherine and Laurence Anholt
- *Jim and the Beanstalk* by Raymond Briggs
- *Oliver's Fruit Salad* by Vivian French
- *Oliver's Vegetables* by Vivian French
- *Alfie and the Birthday Surprise* by Shirley Hughes
- *An Evening at Alfies* by Shirley Hughes
- *Sophie's Tom* by Dick King-Smith

Songs

- *Apusskidu: Songs for Children* chosen by Beatrice Harrop, Peggy Blakeley and David Gadsby
- *Okki-tokki-unga: Action Songs for Children* chosen by Beatrice Harrop, Linda Friend and David Gadsby

Resources for planning

- **England:** Statutory framework for the Early Years Foundation Stage (2012) (www.foundationyears.org.uk/early-years-foundation-stage-2012)
- **Northern Ireland:** CCEA (2011) 'Curricular Guidance for Pre-school Education' (www.rewardinglearning.org.uk/curriculum/pre_school/index.asp). CCEA (2006) Understanding the Foundation Stage (www.nicurriculum.org.uk/docs/foundation_stage/UF_web.pdf)
- **Scotland:** Learning and Teaching Scotland (2010) 'Pre-birth to Three: Positive Outcomes for Scotland's Children and Families' (www.ltscotland.org.uk/earlyyears/). The Scottish Government (2008) 'Curriculum for Excellence: Building the Curriculum 3 – A Framework for Learning and Teaching' (www.ltscotland.org.uk/buildingyourcurriculum/policycontext/btc/btc3.asp)
- **Wales:** Welsh Assembly (2008) 'Framework for Children's Learning for 3 to 7-year-olds in Wales' (http://wales.gov.uk/topics/educationand skills/schoolshome/curriculuminwales/arevised curriculumforwales/foundationphase/?lang=en)

Collecting evidence of children's learning

Monitoring children's development is an important task. Making a profile of children's achievements, strengths, capabilities interests and learning will help you to see progress and will draw attention to those who are having difficulties for some reason. If a child needs additional professional help, such as speech therapy, these cumulative profiles will provide valuable evidence.

Profiles should cover all the areas of learning, as defined by the relevant UK framework, and be the result of collaboration between practitioners, parents and carers. Parents should be made aware of your record keeping policies when their child joins your group. Show parents the types of documentation that you are keeping and make sure they understand their purpose. As a general rule, documentation should be open. Families should have access to their child's documentation at any time and know they can contribute to it. Take regular opportunities to talk to parents about children's progress. If you have formal discussions regarding children about whom you have particular concerns, a dated record of the main points should be kept.

Keeping it manageable

Documentation should be helpful in informing practitioners, adult helpers and parents and always be for the benefit of the child. The golden rule is to keep it simple, manageable and useful. Do not try to make records following every activity!

Documentation will basically fall into two categories – observations and reflections:

Observations

- **Spontaneous observations:** Sometimes you will want to make a note of observations as they happen e.g. a child is heard counting cars accurately during a play activity, or is seen to play collaboratively for the first time.

- **Planned observations:** Sometimes you will plan to make observations of children's developing skills within a planned activity. Using the learning opportunity identified for an activity will help you to make appropriate judgments about children's capabilities, strengths and interests, and to record them systematically.

To collect information:

- Talk to children about their activities and listen to their responses.
- Listen to children talking to each other.
- Observe children's work such as early writing, drawings, paintings and models. (Keeping photocopies or photographs can be useful in tracking progress. Photographs are particularly useful to monitor children's development in the outdoor environment.)

Sometimes it may be appropriate to set up 'one off' activities for the purposes of monitoring development. Some groups at the beginning of each term, for example, ask children to write their name and to make a drawing of themselves to record their progressing skills in both co-ordination and observation.

Reflections

It is useful to spend regular time reflecting on the children's progress. Aim to make some comments about each child each week, and discuss these regularly with colleagues and families.

Informing your planning

Collecting evidence about children's progress is time consuming and it is important that it is useful. When planning, use the information collected to help you to decide what learning opportunities you need to provide next for each child. For example, a child who has poor pencil or brush control will benefit from more play with dough or construction toys to build strength of muscles in the hands and fingers.

Example observation sheet

Name: Lucy Field

Date: 17.1.13

Area of Learning: Mathematics. Count reliably with numbers from 1 to 20.

Context (Please tick):

Child-initiated: √   Adult-led:

Alone: In a group: √

Observation: Lucy is playing outside with two friends. She is trying to build the tallest tower and counting the bricks. "1, 2, 3, 4, 5, 7, 8. Mine's 8. Yours is only 7." She knocks the tower down, chuckles and starts to build again, counting as she places the bricks. "1, 2, 3, 4, 5, 7." The tower falls over. "Oh blow. I wanted to do 20."

What next: Check Lucy knows 6 follows 5. Encourage use of the outdoor counting grids, skittles and number rhyme CD.

Observer: E. M. Hogg

Overview of areas covered through 'People who help us'

	Communication and Language	Physical Development	Personal, Social and Emotional Development	Literacy	Mathematics	Understanding the World	Expressive Arts and Design
People who help us at home	Listening and attention Understanding Speaking	Moving and handling Health and self-care	Self-confidence and self-awareness Managing feelings and behaviour Making relationships	Reading Writing	Numbers Shape, space and measures	People and communities The world Technology	Exploring and using media and materials Being imaginative
People who help us at nursery/school/pre-school	Listening and attention Understanding Speaking	Moving and handling Health and self-care	Self-confidence and self-awareness Managing feelings and behaviour Making relationships	Reading Writing	Numbers Shape, space and measures	People and communities The world Technology	Exploring and using media and materials Being imaginative
People who help us keep us safe	Listening and attention Understanding Speaking	Moving and handling Health and self-care	Self-confidence and self-awareness Managing feelings and behaviour Making relationships	Reading Writing	Numbers Shape, space and measures	People and communities The world Technology	Exploring and using media and materials Being imaginative
People who help us keep us healthy	Listening and attention Understanding Speaking	Moving and handling Health and self-care	Self-confidence and self-awareness Managing feelings and behaviour Making relationships	Reading Writing	Numbers Shape, space and measures	People and communities The world Technology	Exploring and using media and materials Being imaginative
People who help us to have food	Listening and attention Understanding Speaking	Moving and handling Health and self-care	Self-confidence and self-awareness Managing feelings and behaviour Making relationships	Reading Writing	Numbers Shape, space and measures	People and communities The world Technology	Exploring and using media and materials Being imaginative
The Thank You Party	Listening and attention Understanding Speaking	Moving and handling Health and self-care	Self-confidence and self-awareness Managing feelings and behaviour Making relationships	Reading Writing	Numbers Shape, space and measures	People and communities The world Technology	Exploring and using media and materials Being imaginative

Note: For each theme, highlight the Early Learning Goal areas covered through both adult focused and child-initiated activities relating to 'People who help us'.

Home links

The theme of People who help us lends itself to useful links with children's homes and families. Through working together children and adults gain respect for each other and build comfortable and confident relationships.

Establishing partnerships

- Keep parents informed about the activities planned for People who help us, the themes for each week and the proposed date for the thank you party. By understanding the work of the group, parents will enjoy the involvement of contributing ideas, time and resources.
- Photocopy the family page for each child to take home.
- Invite friends, childminders and families to join in the thank you party.

Visiting enthusiasts

- Invite adults to come to the group to talk about how they help people. Remember to include a range of professions, people who work in the home and those who children see each day. Ensure that the visitors are well briefed so that children are enthused.